IELTS ACADEMIC WRITING

How To Write 8+ Answers For The IELTS Exams!

(With High Scoring Sample Answers For Each Question Type)

By Daniella Moyla

IELTS Academic Writing

How To Write 8+ Answers For The IELTS Exam!

Published by Sanbrook Publishing

ISBN-13: 978-1545246245

*****

Table of Contents

WHO IS THIS BOOK FOR?

The IELTS (Academic) can be a very daunting exam in which to achieve a high score. The significance of the IELTS can be the difference between obtaining a visa or position at a university for many people.

Therefore, it is important that if you require a specific IELTS score, you review what makes high quality writing answers before you take the exam.

All too many people take the IELTS several times without reaching their desired score and do not understand why.

This book has been written specifically for people like you who want to view sample writing answers that comply with the standards of the IELTS scoring criteria and would achieve a high score if written for an IELTS exam.

Many sample answers on the internet today are not quality reviewed and can be misleading.

The answers you will find in this book, however, have been written by a professional IELTS teacher with more than 10 years experience who has used these methods to reach high scoring results with most of her students.

If you want to succeed on the IELTS Writing section, then this book will assist you in understanding what is required.

You should read this book if:

- You have taken the IELTS exam before and did not obtain a high score in the writing section and don't know why.

- You have searched the internet for sample answers but you are unsure of the quality of the answers and who wrote them.

- You have never taken the IELTS exam and you want to review how high scoring answers are structured, so you can follow a similar format.

- Your IELTS exam is very soon and you need last minute guidance on how to write high scoring answers.

ACADEMIC WRITING SECTION

The Writing section of the IELTS has two formats, Academic and General Training.

This book refers to the **Academic format**, which is often, but not exclusively, one of the entry requirements for candidates interested in completing tertiary education programmes in most English speaking countries.

The writing section assesses a person's ability to communicate in written English, in an academic context as well as the capacity to understand different tasks and respond to them with an adequate level of accuracy.

Writing Section		
Task	One: Report	Two: Essay
Duration	20 minutes	40 minutes
Word Count	150 words	250 words
Description	Candidates are requested to analyse data presented in the form of a diagram (graph, process or map) and write a report selecting and summarizing the most important features.	Candidates are given a question which needs to be answered in an essay format.

Even though there is an allocation of time for each task, candidates are responsible for managing it, as one hour is given to complete the whole writing section. Which means, that if a candidate spends more than twenty minutes in task 1, he/she will have less time to write the essay which will be detrimental for the final result.

It is also important to remember that task 2 (the essay) is worth double the marks, and hence requires more attention given its level of complexity.

TASK 1 WRITING ACADEMIC

What Is Task 1?

This task in particular, evaluates a candidate's ability to understand data presented in a pictorial diagram. Once the information has been analysed and understood, candidates are expected to write a report explaining the given data.

The illustrations will vary in format, and only one will be given per test. These can include the following:

a) Line graph, chart or table

b) Process or diagram

c) Maps

Suggested Answer Structure (Task 1)

The structure for the report may vary according to the type of illustration received. Generally speaking, the report will be divided in four paragraphs.

Report Structure	
Introduction	This paragraph should not be very long and it mainly consists of a brief paraphrase of the question. Only general information should be included without details or analysis of the data.

Overview	This is the most important paragraph as it is the analysis of the information presented. A highlight of the main trends, stages or differences should be included here.
Detailed Paragraph	This paragraph should include all other details, grouping information as much as possible.
Summary	This paragraph is a restatement of the main trends. In other words it should be a short paraphrase of the overview.

Scoring Criteria (Task 1)

Task 1 is assessed according to four areas which determine the final score in bands from 1 to 9. A brief description of each criterion is provided below:

Scoring Criteria Task 1	
Task achievement	This criterion assesses how well and accurately the information presented in the illustration is reported, and how well main features are highlighted.
Cohesion and Coherence	This criterion assesses how well ideas are sequenced, connected, and organized.
Lexical resource	This criterion assesses the variety of vocabulary and level of sophistication used.
Grammatical range and accuracy	This criterion assesses the variety of structures used and how well they are used in terms of the frequency of errors.

The public version of the Writing scoring criteria is available on www.ielts.org

Task 1 Question Types

A variety of charts can be included in this part of the writing section, however, there is only one per test. Even though graphs are still the most common figure, maps have recently gained a certain level of popularity.

Graphs, Charts & Tables

In this type, a series of numerical features is presented. The main purpose is to identify the trend (rising, falling) as well as to establish comparisons when relevant (the highest, lowest etc.)

Processes

In this type, a sequence of stages or the process of how something works is illustrated in a pictorial diagram. The objective is to identify the steps and functionality of the diagram.

Maps

This is a rather newer type, in which two maps which show the same place with a series of changes are provided. Another possibility is to receive one map where the aim is to compare two different locations for a certain purpose.

Planning Task 1 Reports

One of the main reasons people fail to get a high score in task 1, is due to the lack of planning. This means that most people study the image quickly and start writing the report immediately, which usually results in mistakes such as not providing important details or missing information.

Therefore, it is vital to have a system to follow for task 1 that provides better results.

Steps to follow:

Step 1 - Study the illustration carefully

Read the question a couple of times to make sure you understand what the task is about. Then study the data carefully looking for similarities and differences that will help you determine the main trends, stages or changes.

Step 2 - Make a list of features

Use the page where the illustration is to make a short list of the aspects that will be part of the description. By doing this, you will avoid leaving information out and you will better present your overview.

Step 3 - Write the report for the reader and not for you

This sounds rather obvious, but a common mistake people make in this task, is to write the report assuming the reader will be looking at the illustration simultaneously. This is a mistake because the purpose of the report is that the reader does not feel the need to look at the image because everything described well enough that such action would be unnecessary.

Step 4 - Check and edit your report

Always leave a few minutes at the end to read your report and make any changes necessary before you submit it. Most people understand this is important but usually run out of time before they get a chance to do it. The reality is, you should always have some minutes to spare. If you do not, that means you need more practice.

(handwritten notes in margin)
- read
- plan
- follow the ST
- create o system

Quick Tips For Task 1

1) Have a system and manage your time wisely.

As explained above, most people do not have a system for any of the writing tasks. This is because most people are not used to the idea of planning at all and they think of it as a waste of time.

However, planning is vital in order to get good results. There is no perfect method for planning, but a good place to start is to follow the suggestions above.

Twenty minutes seem to be not enough time for planning, writing and checking. But once more, having a system will help you get there. Keep track of how long it takes you to analyse a graph, take notes and write it.

Use that to create your own system and then practice as much as possible keeping records of the time you spend on each step. After a few trials you will see amazing results.

2) Get familiar with the scoring criteria

Understanding what examiners expect to find in your report is essential. Even though the band descriptors are available on the IELTS official website, not many people have taken the time to try to understand what they actually are and how examiners use them.

But if you do not know what getting an 8 means, then how will you ever get there?

This is not rocket science. The descriptors are quite clear and though they might sound somewhat technical at times, even knowing the main aim of each criterion will help you realize what examiners need to see in order to score you handsomely.

For example, in order to get a 7, you need to at least:

Task achievement

- Write at least 150 words and submit a finished report

- Present an overview that clearly highlights the main trends/stages or changes depicted in the graphic

- Describe all features, though some could be better covered

Cohesion and Coherence

- Present the information in a logical sequence where ideas progress at ease

- Use a range of cohesive devices (linking words, pronoun reference etc.) with some flexibility, though there may be some under/over-use

Lexical range and accuracy

- Use a variety of expressions with some level of sophistication (uncommon words) and some awareness of style and collocation (combination of words such as *"do business"*).

- Make a few errors throughout (most sentences are error-free) in terms of spelling, word choice and form.

Grammatical range and accuracy

- Use a variety of structures with a high level of accuracy (most sentences are error-free) and good control over punctuation.

As it can be seen, a report that gets a 7 is far from being perfect, but it needs to have a high level of accuracy in all four criteria.

In order to get 8, the requirements are the same but there is less room for error and higher expectations in terms of the proficiency in the use of vocabulary and grammar.

3) Paraphrasing is key

Given that the content of task 1 (academic) is provided in the task, paraphrasing is essential on order to show your own understanding of the illustration without having to repeat terms used in the question.

Clearly, there will be words that cannot be replaced, but ideally, most of the information should be grouped or replaced by a synonym or a different expression.

HIGH SCORING TASK 1 SAMPLE ANSWERS

Graph – Sample 1

Question:

You should spend about 20 minutes on this task.

> *The graph below shows the percentage of Australian people giving money to charities in the years 1980 and 2015.*
>
> *Summarise the information by selecting and reporting the main features, and make comparisons where relevant.*

Write at least 150 words.

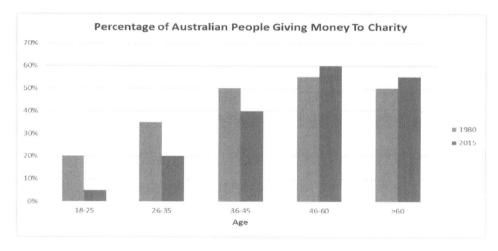

Planning:

Quickly observe the graph and take notes of the main trends and differences and decide what information to describe in each paragraph. (*See example below*)

Introduction:
- Bar graph
- % Australian people donating money to charities by age group
- In years 1980 and 2015

Overview:
- 1980 Highest % = 46-60 yrs 55% / Lowest = 18-25 yrs 20%
- 2015 Highest % = 46-60 yrs 60% / Lowest = 18-25 yrs 5%

Details:
- 1980 had the highest % of donations, except with 46-60 yrs + 60 yrs that increased in 2015
- 2015 had a much lower % of donations across the board.

Sample Answer 1:

introduction

The bar graph represents the percentage of Australian people, arranged by age group, who donated their money to charities, in the years 1980 and 2015. — *ce reprezintă graficul*

overview

It is clear to see that both years showed the same age groups which donated the most and the least to charities, however 2015 had a noticeable decrease. *~~as seabound~~ (prezentare de ansamblu rescurt)*

detailed paragraph

In the year 1980, the two lowest contributors were people aged 18 to 25, at a 20% and people who were 26 to 35 years of age contributing around 35% of their money. (However), in 2015, there were three age groups which showed a much lower percentage of donations, being less than 5%, for people 18 to 25 years of age, followed by a 20% from people aged 26 to 35 and 40% representing people aged 36 to 45. The highest percentage of donations remained in the same age groups both years, represented by the people aged 46 to 60 in and 60 plus, where there was an increase of about 5% in 2015 in comparison to the 50% and 55% observed in 1980. *descriere*

Summary

In summary, it can be concluded that people donate less money to charities in recent years and that as people get older they tend to donate more of their money. *concluzie*

(207 words)

— ce reprezintă graficul (ce vrea el)
— prezentare pe scurt a graficului
— Prezentare detaliată a graficului
— Concluzia

(However) *(in summary)*

Graph – Sample 2

Question:

You should spend about 20 minutes on this task.

The graph below shows the percentage of Canadian people consuming fast food over the decades from 1970 to 2010.

Summarise the information by selecting and reporting the main features, and make comparisons where relevant.

Write at least 150 words.

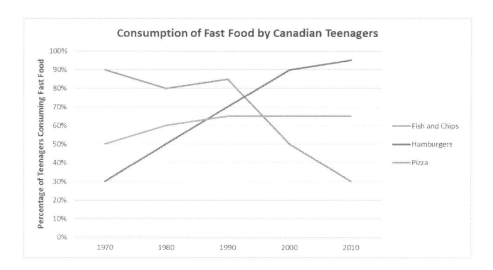

Planning:

Quickly observe the graph and take notes of the main trends and differences and decide what information to describe in each paragraph. *(See example below)*

Introduction:
- Line graph
- % Canadian people consuming fast food (fish and chips, hamburgers and pizza)

Overview:
- There are three main movements, remained almost same (pizza), had huge decrease (fish and chips) and huge increase in consumption (hamburgers)

Details:
- Pizza steady from 50% to 60% and remained same
- Fish and chips started high and plummeted in 2010
- Burguers started low and sky rocketed in 2010

Sample Answer 2:

The line graph shows the percentage of Canadian teenagers who consumed fast food, out of three categories, in five decades from 1970 to 2010.

Overall, it can be seen that there are main movements. The first category, fish and chips, experiences an outstanding decrease the five decades. The second food type, pizza, remains constant with only slight changes and the last food category sky rockets in consumption levels.

Fish and chips seemed to be the most popular fast food type in the 70s when its consumption was as high as 90% but plummeted steadily over the years to reach the lowest point in 2010 at 30%. On the other hand, hamburgers had a slow start at 30% consumption and only became the preferred food in recent years becoming the highest consumed in 2010 at 95%. Finally, pizza was the average favourite increasing from 50% to about 65% in the mid 80s plateauing from then onwards.

In summary, it seems that teenagers' taste has changed over the years but pizza remains a classic.

(172 words)

Process – Sample 1

Question:

You should spend about 20 minutes on this task.

> *The diagram below shows the process of a beer brewery.*
>
> *Summarise the information by selecting and reporting the main features, and make comparisons where relevant.*

Write at least 150 words.

Planning:

Quickly observe the graph and take notes of the main trends and differences and decide what information to describe in each paragraph. *(See example below)*

Introduction:
- Brewery process
- Show complete process from milling to distribution

Overview:
- Linear steps with no options or variations
- Beer is always the same at the end of the process

Details:
- Starts with adding malted barley
- Sugar is added at the boiling stage
- Last step is filtering after which the beer is packaged and distributed

Sample Answer 1:

The diagram illustrates the process undertaken in a beer brewery. The process outlines the steps from the initial milling right through to packaging and distribution.

The process is divided into several linear steps whereby there are no optional steps or variations.

The first part of the brewery process is where the malted barley is introduced to the milling step and is then mashed. At this point water is added where the lautering step occurs. The mixture is then boiled and sugar is added to the blend. Once this happens it is now passed through the whirlpooling step and cooled after. The next part of the process is the fermenting maturing stages. Once the mixture passes through these steps, it is then filtered ready for packaging. The beer is parcelled into different types of containers ready for distribution by lager lorries.

The brewery process includes several different but clear steps meaning the process is relatively straight forward. There are no variations or parts where the process can go two different ways which means the beer is always the same at the end of the brewery process.

(185 words)

Process – Sample 2

Question:

You should spend about 20 minutes on this task.

The diagram below shows the sewage management process at The Altona Treatment Plant.

Summarise the information by selecting and reporting the main features, and make comparisons where relevant.

Write at least 150 words.

Planning:

Quickly observe the graph and take notes of the main trends and differences and decide what information to describe in each paragraph. *(See example below)*

Introduction:
- Treatment plant process
- Shows how sewage is treated

Overview:
- Process shows clear linear steps
- Only variation is at the end

Details:
- Process starts with sewage added to water tank
- Passes through filtration steps
- Can either be used as irrigation recycled water or industrial recycled water

Sample Answer 2:

The illustration outlines the sewage handling process undertaken at The Altona Treatment Plant.

The process includes several steps showing how sewage is treated to be then used as irrigation recycled water or industrial recycled water.

The first part of the sewage management process is where the sewage is added to the feed water tank. Once this occurs the sewage is then passed through screening filters and ultra-filtration modules. After these two filtration steps, the sewage is put through a high pressure pump. At this point the sewage goes through reverse osmosis, First Pass, where the sewage can then be used at irrigation recycled water, for example on golf courses. In order for the sewage to be used as industrial recycled water it must also go through the reverse osmosis, Second Pass, step.

The Altona Treatment Plant Process for treating sewage is not an overly complicated process as it includes clear and direct steps. The only deviation may occur at the end of the process where the treated sewage can either be used as irrigation recycled water or industrial recycled water depending on where the sewage is treated.

(187 words)

Map – Sample 1

Question:

You should spend about 20 minutes on this task.

> *The two maps below show a town in 1995 and then in 2015.*
>
> *Summarise the information by selecting and reporting the main features, and make comparisons where relevant.*

Write at least 150 words.

Planning:

Quickly observe the graph and take notes of the main trends and differences and decide what information to describe in each paragraph. *(See example below)*

Introduction:
- Two maps of same area
- One dated 1995 and other 2015

Overview:
- More development has occurred than not

Details:
- Woodland area has become an adventure park
- Houses area has expanded but park size has reduced
- Hospital, railway station and river all remained the same

Sample Answer 1:

The image shows two maps of the same area, however one map is dated 1995 and the other 2015.

There are several differences in how the area has changed through development over time, but there are also buildings which have remained intact from 1995 to 2015.

Starting at the northern section of both maps, it is clear that the woodland area has now become an Adventure Park. In addition, the housed area has expanded but the park has reduced in size over time. The large house has been developed into a hotel and golf course and there is also a new school above the river. The school has also changed and is now a shopping complex and the public garden has now become factories and warehouses. Lastly, the original street of houses is now apartment blocks. It is important to note that the hospital, railway station and river have all remained the same from 1995 to 2015.

Over time, it is clear that further development has occurred between over 20 years in the map area.

(175 words)

Map – Sample 2

Question:

You should spend about 20 minutes on this task.

> *The map below shows the town Springvale. The local council is proposing to build a playground and there are two possible sites, X1 and X2.*
>
> *Summarise the information by selecting and reporting the main features, and make comparisons where relevant.*

Write at least 150 words.

Planning:

Quickly observe the graph and take notes of the main trends and differences and decide what information to describe in each paragraph. *(See example below)*

Introduction:
- Map of a town
- X1 and X2 are two possible sites for a playground

Overview:
- X1 and X2 are positioned in opposites sides of the town
- Both have good and bad features

Details:
- X1 is located in quieter residential area
- X2 is located close to a railway station and a car park
- Neither site is close to the school

Sample Answer 2:

The map illustrates two possible sites where the council is looking to build a playground in the town of Springvale.

It is firstly evident that the two sites are on opposite sides of the town and have very different infrastructure surrounding each site. X1 site is positioned in the north western area of the town and X2 site is positioned in the eastern area of the town.

It can be observed that the X1 site is located in the quieter residential area surrounded by apartment buildings, houses and a lake. On the other hand, X2 site is very close to a railway station and a car park with as well as a factory nearby. The X2 site is also located next to a road, whereas X1 is more isolated away from traffic. Neither site is close to the school nor fall under the flight path of planes.

The proposed sites for the playground are located in very different areas with both good and bad features for a playground, but it can be stated that X1 might be a slighter better option considering it is closer to the residential zone.

(189 words)

TASK 2 WRITING ACADEMIC

What Is Task 2?

Task 2 consists of a question about general knowledge that needs to be answered in the form of an essay. There are no major differences between the General Training and Academic formats for task 2, except that the topics used in the questions may vary slightly, where themes such as *"Education"* or *"Environmental issues"* are more likely to appear in the Academic format, rather than *"TV"*, or *"Technology"* that may be more common in the General Training format.

There are three main question types in this part of the writing section:

a) Opposing-views question (Argument)

b) Opinion-based question (Proposal)

c) Two-part question (Discussion)

Suggested Answer Structure (Task 2)

The structure for the essay may vary somewhat according to the type of question provided, but generally speaking, the essay should be divided into four paragraphs.

Essay Structure	
Introduction	This paragraph should not be very long and it mainly consists of a brief paraphrase of the question. Important details to include are: - **The topic of the question** What is the essay about? Example: *"The use of mobile phones"* - **The outline of the essay or Thesis Statement** What aspects of the topic will be covered in the essay? Example: *"Advantages and disadvantages"*
First body paragraph	Each body paragraph will have the same structure: - **Topic sentence** The summary of the paragraph in one sentence Example: *"There are many advantages to using mobile phones for communication."* - **Explanation** What proves the topic sentence Example: *"One advantage is that using a cell phone allows people to communicate with others at anytime and anywhere."* - **Example(s)** What provides evidence for the explanation

	Example:
	"For instance, if I get lost, I can contact my mother using my mobile in order to get instructions of how to get home from where I am."
Second body paragraph	Same as above ▪ **Topic sentence** ▪ **Explanation** ▪ **Example(s)**
Conclusion	A restatement of what the essay described or dealt with and a brief summary of the main points should be included. Example: "To sum up, both pros and cons can be found when discussing the use mobile phones in terms of..."

Scoring Criteria (Task 2)

Task 2 is assessed according to four areas which determine the final score in bands from 1 to 9. A brief description of each criterion is provided below:

Scoring Criteria Task 2	
Task response	This criterion assesses how well and thoroughly the question has been answered, as well as how much evidence is provided in the essay's development.

Cohesion and Coherence	This criterion assesses how well ideas are sequenced, connected, and organized. It also evaluates the use of Topic Sentences and paragraph structure.
Lexical resource	This criterion assesses the variety of vocabulary and level of sophistication and accuracy used.
Grammatical range and accuracy	This criterion assesses the variety of grammatical structures used and how well they are used in terms of the frequency of errors.

*The public version of the Writing scoring criteria is available on www.ielts.org

As it can be seen, there are no major variances between the scoring criteria for task 1 and 2. The main discrepancies are found in the first and second criteria, where the focus is on the content of the response and the structure used in Task 2.

Task 2 Question Types

Opposing-Views Question (formerly known as Argument)

Description

This question type refers to the cases where candidates are asked to analyse two sides of a topic/problem and present a personal opinion.

There are two cases in this question type:

Case 1) Advantage/disadvantage

In this case, a topic is given and the question asks to examine the advantages and disadvantages of it. An important aspect is that the development of the essay needs to impartial and the personal opinion should be stated at the end (conclusion) of the response.

Example:

> *Modern technology is being used more and more in different aspects of our lives, such as education. Do the **advantages** of using technology as an educational tool outweigh its **disadvantages**?*

Case 2) Some people say …/While others believe…

This case can be confusing because they will present two points of view or perspectives regarding the same topic. Most people think they are allowed to choose one side and describe that side only in their response, but contrary to that belief, candidates are requested to discuss both views (objectively) and then provide a personal position.

Example:

> ***Some people** believe that exams are essential to measure students' learning outcomes, **while others** believe that these assessments are unnecessary and unfair. What is your opinion?*

Opinion-Based Question (formerly known as Proposal)

This question type refers to the cases where candidates are asked to take a side regarding the statement presented in the question and provide their personal opinion about it. The difference between this question type and the former, is that in this case, candidates are free to choose the side they want to support, whereas in the *"opposing-views question type"*, both sides need to be analysed before an opinion is presented.

There are three cases in this question type:

Case 1) What is your opinion?

This case can seem rather ambiguous because the question itself is not very specific. A typical scenario is when a strong statement is provided and then an opinion is requested.

Example:

> *More money should be spent on hiring and training the police force in order to reduce crime in big cities. What is **your opinion**?*

Case 2) Do you agree or disagree?

This case is easy to identify because the question is always worded in the same way, by using the terms **agree** or **disagree**.

Example:

> *Sports are the only way to keep youngsters out trouble and should be encouraged from an early age. Do you **agree** or **disagree** with this statement?*

Case 3) To what extent do you agree or disagree?

This case is exactly the same as the previous one, but some people think that because the question is worded differently, they are being asked a different question. This is not the situation at all, it is just an alternative way to ask the same, which is the candidate's agreement towards the statement. The words used are: **To what extent** do you agree of disagree?

Example:

> *Children's leisure activities should always be educational because they have too much to learn before they become adults.* **To what extent** do you **agree** or **disagree**?

In other words, these three cases, reflect the same aim, which is to express agreement or disagreement in regards to the statement presented in the question.

A common misconception about these three cases is that some people believe the following:

> ➢ When the question is directly: **do you agree or disagree?**, the only possible answer can either be <u>full agreement or disagreement</u>. This is not true.

> ➢ When the question states: **to what extent do you agree or disagree?** the only possible answer is to <u>partly agree</u>. Again, untrue.

The truth is, that regardless of the question received, if it belongs to the Opinion-based type, there are three possible answers:

I.   Total agreement

II. Partial agreement

III. Total disagreement

In my experience, I can say that in most circumstances, a safer option is usually to partially agree. This is because choosing this option, would provide more arguments to include in the body paragraphs. When total agreement or disagreement are presented, the development tends to be quite narrow, and therefore weak.

Two-Part Question (formerly known as Discussion)

This question type refers to the cases in which candidates are given a problem or issue and are asked to discuss two questions/aspects about it. In other words, there are two parts to the question, hence the name.

There are two cases in this question type:

Case 1) Causes + Solutions or Effects

This case is easy to identify because the question is reasonably direct. It usually asks to explain the reasons that have produced a certain problem, and to provide suggestions/solutions or to discuss the effects this problem brings.

Example:

> In many countries there has been a noticeable increase of road accidents. What do you think are the **causes** of this? What **solutions** can you suggest?

Note that in this case, *"causes and effects"* or *"causes and solutions"* of a problem, there are two formats that can be used in the answer:

1) **Chain structure**: This is when one cause and one effect/solution are described in the same paragraph. The objective of this structure, is to present the ideas that are related. For example:

Causes and effects of pollution

> **Cause:** use of cars **+ Solution:** people should use public transport more

2) **Block structure**: This structure is used when all the *causes* are described in one paragraph, and all the *effects/solutions* are dealt with in another paragraph. For example:

Causes and effects of pollution

> **Causes:**
> 1) use of cars
> 2) factory emissions
>
> **Solutions:**
> 1) people should be more eco-friendly
> 2) government should tax industries and car users

This structure is recommended when the *causes* and *effects/solutions* do not necessarily correlate each other. (*See samples provided below*)

Case 2) Question 1 + Question 2

This case can be more difficult to identify. The best way to recognize it is to count the number of questions being asked. The difference between this case and the former, is that in this instance, the questions are not necessarily related to each other. On the contrary, they are usually fairly independent from each other.

Example:

> *In some countries, the tenancy and use of fire arms is allowed for most people.* ***Do you think*** *that other countries should follow this trend?* ***What problems*** *could this bring?*

In summary, this question type requires candidates to discuss the two parts to the question in different body paragraphs. Each pat of the question should be dealt with independently.

Task 2 Question Types Summary

As explained above, there are mainly three question types in task 2. Many names have been given to these question categories, and the names do not really matter if the question is not answered correctly.

In my previous book, I called them: **Argument, Proposal** and **Discussion**. I have included those names in brackets () in this book, in order to help readers identify them better.

New names have been given this time, with the purpose making the categories more self-explanatory.

What this approach aims to do, is to provide a clear way to identify what questions request to do in order to maximize the score received in Task Response.

Therefore, three main categories have been described, each one proposing a different objective.

Task 2 Question Types (Mind Map)

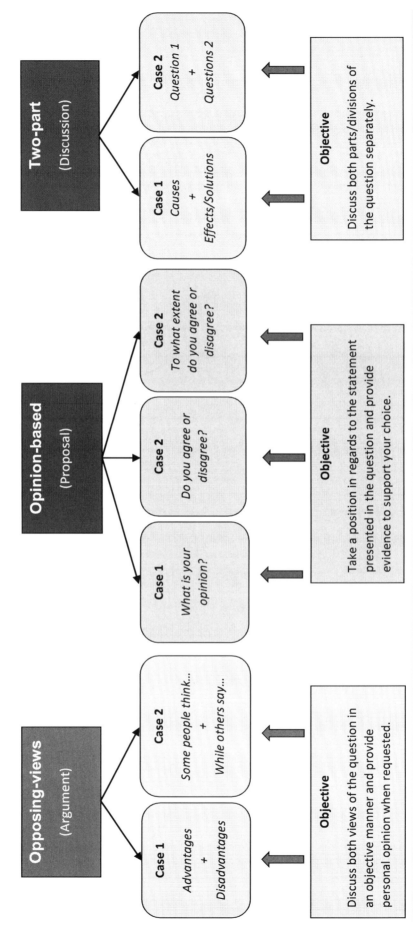

Opposing-views (Argument)

Case 1
Advantages
+
Disadvantages

Case 2
Some people think...
+
While others say...

Objective
Discuss both views of the question in an objective manner and provide personal opinion when requested.

Opinion-based (Proposal)

Case 1
What is your opinion?

Case 2
Do you agree or disagree?

Case 2
To what extent do you agree or disagree?

Objective
Take a position in regards to the statement presented in the question and provide evidence to support your choice.

Two-part (Discussion)

Case 1
Causes
+
Effects/Solutions

Case 2
Question 1
+
Questions 2

Objective
Discuss both parts/divisions of the question separately.

Planning Task 2 Essays

Planning essays is a step that most people try to avoid, because they think it is unnecessary and a waste of time. In my years helping people prepare for the IELTS, I have only encountered a small minority of students who understand how important planning is.

The biggest mistake is to think planning is optional. The reality is, that without a plan, people keep making the same mistakes over and over again which explains why some people hit a roof with their Writing score and cannot move forward.

I have had many students who come to me with a 6.5 in Writing and no matter how much they practice, they cannot seem to make any progress. In most cases their problem, is either the lack of planning, or planning incorrectly.

In other words, planning can be the difference between obtaining the desired score or not, so here is what needs to be understood about planning:

- **It is not a waste of time**. It is actually quite the contrary. Planning is an investment that in the long run, helps us save time. By having a clear plan of what we want to write, in the order we want to write it, with the examples we will use to support our ideas, we will save a big amount of time when we actually start writing and the process will be much smoother.

- **It is not, or at least it should not be, optional**. The main result that comes from not planning is having lack of unity, improvising and shifting in focus.

- **It should not take too long**, and it should be done in a key word system to avoid wasting time. Writing full sentences in a plan is definitely a waste of time, consequently, we should stick to concepts/key word that represent a whole patch of writing.

- **The more it is done, the faster/easier it becomes**. Like everything else in life, practice makes perfect.

Thus, it is vital to have a planning method to follow for task 2 that provides better results.

Steps to follow:

1) **Analize the question carefully**

   Too many people lose valuable points in Task Response due to not answering the question properly, which is usually a result of not studying the question carefully. When reading the question there are two factors to consider:

   a) *What type of question is it?*

      This is very important because by identifying the question type, the approach to use in the answer should be clear as well (objective, personal etc). This will increase the chances of getting a good score in Task Response.

   b) *What is the Topic of the question?*

      All questions have a common topic and sometimes sub-topics that need to be identified before starting the essay, otherwise the question will not be addressed fully.

This step should take between 2 to 3 minutes.

2) Chose what to plan for

Depending on how much practice a person has or how quickly someone can come up with ideas, there might be more or less to plan for. In general, a couple of ideas should be considered for the introduction, as well as the topic sentence for each body paragraph and the arguments and examples that will be provided in these paragraphs. Generally, planning for the conclusion is not necessary because this paragraph should be a summary of what has already been stated throughout the essay (see *Suggested answer structure* above). This step should take between 8 to 10 minutes.

What to plan for?

Introduction
What is the topic of the question?
What is the essay about?
First Body Paragraph
Topic Sentence
Argument 1 + Example
(Optional) Argument 2 + Example
Second Body Paragraph
Topic Sentence
Argument 1 + Example
(Optional) Argument 2 + Example

3) Write the essay

Once a good plan has been drafted, it is time to start writing. Ideally, this step should be as smooth and uninterrupted as possible to allow for flow. The more people stop while writing, the more disjointed ideas get. This step should take between 23 to 25 minutes to allow enough time for checking.

4) Check and edit your essay

And again, this should not be an optional *"if I have time" step*, but rather a compulsory part of the process that ensures a good end result. When editing, it is important to check if all ideas are clear, well-connected and organized. Most people just try to quickly fix their grammar errors but forget the other aspects being assessed. This step should take between 3 to 5 minutes.

Quick Tips For Task 2

1) Have a system and manage your time wisely.

There are a few external factors in the IELTS that we have absolute no control over. For instance, we cannot choose the question we will get, or the examiner that will mark our essay.

But there are some factors that we do have total control over, such as having a system. We can control how much we practice, what method to plan we use, how much we read in order to get ideas for our essays and how we manage our time.

Having a clear vision of how to tackle the writing, and in this case the essay, will help us boost our confidence and minimize the room for error.

2) Get familiar with the scoring criteria

It is nearly impossible not to be familiar with the scoring criteria and get good results. This is because examiners are trained to look for very specific features in IELTS essays.

So in order to tick all their boxes, we need to understand what their expectations are. In the previous chapter, we looked at the scoring criteria for task 1, which does not vary much from Task 2's.

The only criterion that is completely different is the first, which in this case is called Task response. Thus, in order to get a 7, the following needs to occur:

Task response

- Write at least 250 words and submit a finished essay

- Present clear position and provide enough evidence and support, though there may be a tendency to over-generalize.

- Cover all aspects of the question.

Cohesion and Coherence

- Present the information in a logical sequence where ideas progress at ease.

- Use a range of cohesive devices (linking words, pronoun reference etc) with some flexibility, though there may be some under/over-use

- Paragraphing should be adequate where there is good use of topic sentences.

Lexical range and accuracy

- Use a variety of expressions with some level of sophistication (uncommon words) and some awareness of style and collocation.

- Make a few errors throughout (most sentences are error-free) in terms of spelling, word choice and form.

Grammatical range and accuracy

- Have a variety of structures with a high level of accuracy (most sentences are error-free) and good control over punctuation.

As it can be seen, an essay that gets a 7 is far from being perfect, but it needs to have a high level of accuracy in all four criteria.

In order to get an 8, the requirements are the same but there is less scope for inaccuracy and higher expectations in terms of the proficiency and variety in the use of vocabulary and grammar.

3) Practice, practice and practice

The only way to improve in Writing is to practice so much, that it becomes mechanic or second nature. Each individual will have different strengths and weaknesses, but everybody needs to write as many times as possible in order to get better at it.

Reading is also important with the aim to be up-to-date with current affairs that might appear in the essay questions. Once difficulties have been identified, practice needs to be applied in those particular areas until the desired results are achieved.

For example, many of my students complain that it takes them too long to plan. Well, the response I give them is quite obvious, but sometimes the obvious is invisible to us.

I always say: *"Stop writing full essays. Take some time to write just plans. Time yourself. The first plan might take you 15 minutes to draft, the second hopefully 12 and the third maybe 10. It should only get better from there."*

Now that the essay structure, planning and question types have been explained, let us take a look at some model answers.

HIGH SCORING TASK 2 SAMPLE ANSWERS

Opposing-Views Question type

Case 1 - Sample A

Write about the following topic:

Home-schooling has become very popular in recent years. However, most people still believe that attending schools is the best way to obtain a formal education. What are the advantages and disadvantages of home-schooling?

Give reasons for your answer and include any relevant examples from your own knowledge or experience.

Write at least 250 words.

Suggested Plan:

Topic: Home-schooling
Thesis Statement: Pros and Cons

Topic sentence: advantages of home-schooling
- **Advantage 1:** Tailor-made
- **Example:** children learn at their own pace
- **Advantage 2:** Safe environment
- **Example:** No bullying or risk of other dangers

Topic sentence: disadvantages of home-schooling
- **Disadvantage 1:** lack of socialization
- **Example:** children need interaction with peers
- **Disadvantage 2:** no extra-curricular activities
- **Example:** no opportunity to discover talents or skills

The way of parenting has radically changed over the last decade. Different styles have emerged and parents seem much more involved in their children's development. With this new model, many parents have decided to home-school their offspring instead of sending them to school. It is clear to see why this has become a popular new trend, but as in everything else, benefits and drawbacks need to be considered.

Firstly, some rather obvious advantages to home-schooling can be found. One of them, is the fact that the teaching method used either by parents or tutors can be modified to suit the child or children's needs. This means that children are able to learn at their own pace through the application of an approach that has been tailor-made considering their interests and learning styles. This is particularly valuable for children with disabilities or special needs. Additionally, a more secure environment can be provided for the child, where there are no dangers of being bullying or badly influenced by other pupils.

Contrarily, there are also negative aspects to this new trend. To start with, by studying at home children will miss out on a vital aspect of schools which is socialising with other children their age. Interacting with their peers is essential as it will help children develop all sorts of skills such as problem-solving, team work and leadership, all of which are important for the future professional life. Similarly, no matter how much effort parents put into making the home resemble the school environment, they will never be able to match the resources and extra-curricular activities that are available in schools, such as gyms, musical instruments or science laboratories. All of which would allow students to discover their talents and passions.

All in all, it is evident that home-schooling can be a beneficial experience for some children but given the limitations it involves, parents should consider all angles before deciding how to educate their children.

(343 words)

Case 1 - Sample B

Write about the following topic:

Modern technology is being used more and more in different aspects of our lives, such as education. Do the advantages of using technology as an educational tool outweigh its disadvantages?

Give reasons for your answer and include any relevant examples from your own knowledge or experience.

Write at least 250 words.

Suggested Plan:

Topic: Modern technology as educational tool
Thesis Statement: Outweigh Pros and Cons

Topic sentence: advantages of using tech as educational tool • **Advantage 1:** dynamic • **Example:** different resources: videos, apps, interactive books • **Advantage 2:** we live in a high-tech world • **Example:** everyone is exposed to tech devices, that is the future	**Topic sentence:** disadvantages of using tech as educational tool • **Disadvantage 1:** can be distracting • **Example:** counteractive effect • **Disadvantage 2:** over-exposure to screen and tech • **Example:** children are surrounded by screen and tech devices

We currently live in an era in which technology has become an essential part of our lives. These days, even schools have implemented technological resources in the classroom in order to aid teachers. Even though many people would agree that this is a positive practice, negative aspects should to be pondered as well.

Using technology as an educational instrument can definitely be a positive experience for students. First of all, it is undeniable that technology can bring dynamism to the classroom by incorporating an endless number of resources such as videos, applications pupils can use in their computers and even phones, interactive course books and so on, all of which are bound to capture students' attention. Additionally, it is a reality that our world will highly depend on technology in years to come. Which means that, introducing technology in schools may prepare children for their future, as they will certainly be exposed to these tools throughout their lives.

Nevertheless, on the down side of the matter, some drawbacks need to be taken into account. The first issue, is that technology can be quite distracting for students, especially younger ones, who may lack the discipline to focus on what the teacher is doing, and therefore, a counteractive effect can be seen. As a teacher myself, I struggle getting my students to concentrate in class when their phones are constantly beeping or vibrating. Another disadvantage, is that children are already overly exposed to screens, computers and other electric devices that can have a very detrimental effect on their development and can cause some health issues such as eye-sight problems, lack of sleep and even hyper-active behaviour.

In my opinion, it is clear to see that the application of technology in schools can be beneficial for students, but I think the disadvantages outweigh the benefits in terms of the negative effects that children would be exposed to.

(314 words)

Opposing-Views Question type

Case 2 - Sample A

Write about the following topic:

Alcohol consumption has increased dramatically over the years. Some people believe that the government should increase taxes on alcoholic beverages but others oppose to this idea and advocate personal responsibility. What do you think?

Give reasons for your answer and include any relevant examples from your own knowledge or experience.

Write at least 250 words.

Suggested Plan:

Topic: increasing prices for alcoholic beverages
Thesis Statement: advocates and detractors

Topic sentence: reasons to support the price rise
- **Reason 1:** discourage consumption
- **Example:** higher prices might inhibit people from buying alcohol
- **Reason 2:** gov can use the taxes for positive policies
- **Example:** educating people about risks of excessive alcohol

Topic sentence: reasons to be against the measure
- **Reason 1:** free will
- **Example:** people should be able to choose what to do
- **Reason 2:** everyone pays the price
- **Example:** not all of us consume alcohol in big amounts

In today's society, the immoderate use of alcoholic beverages has alarmed governments around the world. This exorbitant consumption brings about all sorts of adverse effects such as street violence, over-dosing, especially among youngsters, and driving offenses. Given this scenario, some authorities have proposed increasing the levy on alcohol, which has divided the public's opinion into advocates and detractors.

It is clear to see why so many citizens would support this initiative. As a first point, this scheme would most likely discourage consumers from purchasing alcohol at a much higher price than they would otherwise pay for these products. Besides, the money collected from this additional tax can be spent on implementing projects that would benefit the entire community, such as educational programmes that aim to create awareness about the risks of uncontrolled use of alcohol, or building rehabilitation centres for those who have become addicted to this substance.

On the other hand, some rather convincing arguments can be found to oppose this policy. One of them, is the idea that the government would be interfering with people's free will by deciding what is better for them. Many people are against this view because they consider that each individual should be free to decide what they want to do with their lives, even if this brings harmful consequences. Also, some argue that by increasing the levy already imposed on alcohol, those who enjoy an occasional drink would pay the price for the reckless consumers, which can be considered an unfair outcome.

To sum up, I believe that ultimately, the government is responsible for protecting its citizens, and if a measure like this results in a decrease in the consumption of a beverage that tis known for altering people's behaviour, usually in a detrimental manner, then I support such intrusion.

(298 words)

Case 2 - Sample B

Write about the following topic:

Some people believe that dangerous criminals should spend the rest of their lives in prison, while others think that everyone deserves a second chance and that these offenders should be reintegrated into society. What is your opinion?

Give reasons for your answer and include any relevant examples from your own knowledge or experience.

Write at least 250 words.

Suggested Plan:

Topic: dangerous criminals
Thesis Statement: should get life sentence or be given another chance

Topic sentence: should spend life in prison
- **Reason 1:** community safety
- **Example:** protect innocent people
- **Reason 2:** repeat offenders
- **Example:** crime becomes a lifestyle

Topic sentence: should be part of society
- **Reason 1:** people can change
- **Example:** everyone makes mistakes
- **Reason 2:** prison can be worse in some cases
- **Example:** mistreatment

In a world where crime seems to gloomily be on the increase, what to do with inmates after they serve their sentence, has become a controversial issue. There are mainly two lines of thought, one that suggests that dangerous criminals should be kept in captivity for the rest of their lives, and those who believe that convicts should be reintegrated to society.

Understandably, those who support life sentence have strong motives to hold that opinion. A common argument, is the fact that law abiding citizens should not be put at risk by allowing minacious felons roam freely after they have served time in jail. It would be fair to say, that most people would react reluctantly towards a person they know has transgressed the law. Another point to consider, is the fact that many studies show that a high percentage of delinquents reoffend soon after they have been released, which would obviously concern many.

On the flip side of the coin, there are always groups of philanthropists that believe in second chances. These people believe that wrongdoing is part of human nature and that regardless of the severity of the crime, this should not define a person forever. Their thought is that everyone makes mistakes and therefore, we should kindly believe that people can change. Another reason to oppose keeping offenders in prison, is the fact that they might be subject to all kinds of abuse and they might even learn how to commit more crimes if they are ever released. As some say, there is no better school than prison.

In my perspective, it is difficult to choose a side in regards to this issue. I think that each case should be treated independently and enough filters should be put in place to make sure that criminals who are freed do not reoffend.

(304 words)

Opinion-based Question type

Case 1 - Sample A

Write about the following topic:

Traffic congestion is a serious problem in most big cities. Some people believe that governments should build more roads. What do you think about this solution?

Give reasons for your answer and include any relevant examples from your own knowledge or experience.

Write at least 250 words.

Suggested Plan:

Topic: traffic congestion
Thesis Statement: building new roads is a good solution with a huge obstacle

Topic sentence: good solution • **Reason 1:** ease congestion • **Example:** Melbourne • **Reason 2:** better connectivity • **Example:** Melbourne	**Topic sentence:** impact on residents • **Reason 1:** land acquisition • **Example:** my grandparents

Most big cities suffer from the increasing problem of excessive traffic. Dwellers in mega metropolises such as Moscow, put up with hours of driving short distances. Some people have suggested that a way to tackle this issue is to construct more roads. I tend to think this is a good solution, although there is an important aspect to consider.

To begin with, this measure would be positive for two main reasons. The first point, is that having additional roads, especially highways, would greatly ease traffic congestion as cars, trucks and buses would be spread out in different areas. Another reason, is that new paths would also allow for better connectivity between suburbs. An illustration of these points is Melbourne, where population has grown substantially over the last few decades and as a result, the use of private cars has picked as well. The provision of new freeways that connect the southern, northern, eastern and western suburbs, allow people to efficiently travel the long distances of this big city.

As an opposite perspective, it is also important to consider the residents who would be severely affected by this developments. As a first argument, in order to build more roads, land acquisition would most likely take place. This means that residents living in the prospective are of construction, lose their properties, and though get compensated for it, would have no choice but to relocate. I witnessed this first hand when my grandparents' house was acquired by the government because it was situated in an area where a new train station was projected. Even though they got remunerated for their property, my grandparents had to leave the house where they raised their children, had a life and planned on staying for the rest of their lives.

All angles considered, I believe that progress sometimes has a high price tag that only a handful pay. For this reason, I think that the need for building new roads has to be justified enough to make it worth it for those who would have leave their homes for the greater good.

(345 words)

Case 1- Sample B

Write about the following topic:

More money should be spent on hiring and training the police force in order to reduce crime in big cities. What is your opinion?

Give reasons for your answer and include any relevant examples from your own knowledge or experience.

Write at least 250 words.

Suggested Plan:

Topic: more training for police force to reduce crime
Thesis Statement: partly agree

Topic sentence: good solution
- **Reason 1:** better to prevent crime

Topic sentence: crime is complex
- **Reason 1:** roots of crime
- **Example:** USA

How to reduce crime is a wildly discussed topic by most authorities, especially around election time. The fact of the matter is that crime has intensified worldwide. Some say that having more and better trained police officers might help reduce delinquency. However, I believe that while this might be the case, the depth of the problem needs to be examined as well.

On one hand, I do think this solution may contribute positively. Clearly, prevention is always a preferred method in any situation. This means that higher numbers of officers on the streets could potentially discourage criminals to break the law, knowing that there is more surveillance and consequently they may run a higher risk of getting caught. Additionally, improved preparation for the police force would better-equip them to foresee criminal activity and stop it before it occurs. For instance, top of the range technology and special training has allowed the stoppage of potential terrorist attacks in Australia.

On the other hand, crime is a very complex issue that requires further consideration. The roots of crime are so varied and intricate that it is hard to imagine that, only having more policemen, would solve the problem. These days the motivations criminals have to act are quite often unpredictable. The lack of social protection and support for vulnerable people is what often leads to illegal activity. A good example of this is the US where millions are invested in the creation of new prisons, but nothing has been done in regard to gun possession even though this is one of the countries with the highest number of mass shootings, which kills and injures hundreds each year.

In sum, I believe that more resources should be spent not only on training and hiring police officers but also providing better welfare for citizens around the world, which in my opinion would be the most efficient method to avert illegal activity.

(317 words)

Case 2- Sample A

Write about the following topic:

It is currently believed that children's behaviour and misconduct is due to the lack of strict discipline and punishment applied by parents. Do you agree or disagree with this statement?

Give reasons for your answer and include any relevant examples from your own knowledge or experience.

Write at least 250 words.

Suggested Plan:

Topic: children's behaviour caused by parent's leniency
Thesis Statement: partly agree

Topic sentence: Agree
- **Reason 1:** parenting models have changed
- **Example:** tantrums at shops

Topic sentence: Disagree
- **Reason 1:** other factors
- **Example:** external influence

It is common to hear experts' concern about the younger generation and their poor behaviour. Some believe that the main cause of this tendency is the lack of discipline applied by parents. Although I believe this is true to certain degree, I also think there are other factors to be considered.

First of all, I believe this this phenomenon has been aggravated by the endless array of information available for parents. New models of parenting have arisen and with these, a sometimes misleading number of strategies on how to parent have become widely accepted. Advice on what to do with children from when they are born to when they become adults is accessible in books, blogs and even hospitals. Practices previous generations applied such as grounding children or using the word "no" to teach them they cannot always get what they want, are now regarded as old-fashioned and even cruel. A good illustration of this is a visit to any shop, where a common scene is to find a crying child and a mortified mother or father who vainly tries to discipline his or her child, but ends up giving in to the child's whim to stop the crying and the strangers' pity looks.

Conversely, some would argue that parents are not the only factor. This is because it is undeniable that regardless of the parents' efforts, children nowadays have access to an assortment of information from a variety of media channels that no other previous generation has experienced before. This would clearly have an impact on the youngsters' behaviour. Additionally, friends are usually one of the biggest influences in a person's life. Therefore, the type of friends our children have would absolutely have an effect on how they act and how they treat others. We have all most likely been victims of peer pressure, and I would say at least from experience, it is nothing to be proud of.

To conclude, I do believe that parents are the primary source of guidance for children. But I also believe that regardless of how hard parents try to teach their children good manners and conduct, there will always be other sources of influence in their lives out of the parents' control.

(370 words)

Case 2- Sample B

Write about the following topic:

Children's leisure activities should always be educational because they have too much to learn before they become adults. Do you agree or disagree?

Give reasons for your answer and include any relevant examples from your own knowledge or experience.

Write at least 250 words.

Suggested Plan:

Topic: children's free time should be educational
Thesis Statement: disagree

Topic sentence: childhood is too short
- **Reason 1:** children need playtime for development
- **Example:** only a quarter of a person's life

Topic sentence: too much emphasis in academic learning
- **Reason 1:** inhibits creativity
- **Example:** children need to find their skills and abilities

In the busy and competitive world we live in, it is common to see parents worry about their children's education much more than in the past. Some say, that all activities infants take part in should have an educational focus in order for them to learn as much as possible before becoming adults. Personally, I tend to disagree with this statement.

To begin with, childhood is one of the shortest stages of a person's life. Many experts have confirmed that children require several hours of pure playtime in order to develop their minds and bodies comprehensively. From the moment they are born, children are ready to explore the world. They will have plenty of time in their future lives to learn the theory of how everything works and be given all sorts of responsibilities. With the expanding life expectancy, almost reaching a hundred these days, it is fair to say that childhood only accounts for about a quarter of a person's life, and this time should be spent discovering the world around them rather than focusing on just learning.

Additionally, I believe far too much emphasis is placed on academic learning. Currently, most countries impose long school regimes in which children must be in class for an average of seven hours a day. After school, they need to attend other chores which usually include more work such as school assignments and projects. This in turn, can inhibit creativity as children are left with virtually no time to discover their talents and abilities which is essential for their happiness. It seems as though governments have lost sight of what the educational system should be about and is creating the concept that Mathematics and Science are more important than Art and Music.

In a nutshell, it is my belief that children should be given more time to be free and do activities they are truly interested in, which will help them discover what they are passionate about. Our job as a society should be to form happy children as opposed to impose learning experiences all the time.

(345 words)

Case 3- Sample A

Write about the following topic:

Sports events such as the Formula One and other car racing events should be banned because they are an unnecessary waste of money and create more pollution. To what extent do you agree or disagree with this statement?

Give reasons for your answer and include any relevant examples from your own knowledge or experience.

Write at least 250 words.

Suggested Plan:

Topic: Banning of sporting events like F1 due to waste of money and pollution
Thesis Statement: Disagree but changes should be made

Topic sentence: Disagree ▪ **Reason 1:** Many people love Formula 1 ▪ **Example:** Buzz, energy and excitement	**Topic sentence:** Take more responsibility ▪ **Reason 1:** Food & drink waste ▪ **Example:** Give left-overs to homeless

Sporting events, such as Formula 1, are incredibly popular across the world and generate enormous interest from fans and the media. However, Formula 1 is known to waste significant sums of money and also create additional pollution than we already have, which is why some say it should be banned. In my opinion, these events should not be prohibited but people behind these sports should take more responsibility for the negative effects these activities have on society and the environment.

Firstly, one argument to oppose this measure is that it would leave numerous people without a passion. Having been to several Formula 1 events, it is not difficult to see the enjoyment that so many people get from following and attending each Formula 1 race. People travel from all over the world to visit races, which not only generates revenue for the local economy, but also brings world attention to each race location. I myself love the exhilaration and energy of the event and love watching the excitement and intensity of the race. I will certainly bring my children to races in the future because it is a really enjoyable day out.

However, this is not to say that the Formula 1 governing body should not take more responsibility for the negative effects it has. The statistics of food and drinks that are provided for each race is incredibly high, but so is the amount of it that goes to waste. For example, it would be a responsible idea for the Formula 1 governing body to give any left-over food to homeless shelters or organisations that help disadvantaged people. In addition, modifying the car engines in order to lower the levels of pollution that the cars emit would also show that they are taking responsibility for the environment.

In summary, even though events like the Formula 1 do have some negative effects, the enjoyment and passion it provides to people all over the world significantly outweighs the negatives. However, anything that the governing body can do to be more accountable for the negative effects, is certainly something that they should be strongly aim to do.

(355 Words)

Case 3- Sample A

Write about the following topic:

Animal testing has always been a controversial issue. Some people believe that governments should ban these practices completely. To what extent do you agree or disagree with this statement?

Give reasons for your answer and include any relevant examples from your own knowledge or experience.

Write at least 250 words.

Suggested Plan:

Topic: The banning of animal testing
Thesis Statement: Partly agree

Topic sentence: Agree
- **Reason 1:** Animals have feelings
- **Example:** rabbits

Topic sentence: Disagree
- **Reason 1:** positive research
- **Example:** immunizations

Testing on animals is a practice that has been conducted for many years and for a variety of reasons. Some people strongly disagree with animal testing and believe that governments should discontinue it altogether. In my opinion, it would be preferable not to test on animals, but there are many reasons to be grateful for the results of this practice.

To begin with, animals that are used for testing all have feelings of pain and discomfort. Many of us choose not to know what actually happens in laboratories where these experiments take place, because it is obvious that this would not be an enjoyable sight. Clearly, the primary reason to experiment on animals is to analyse the way they react to certain substances in order to conclude whether these would be safe for humans. Consequently, it is only expectable that animals that are tested on would experience a huge amount of stress, pain and anxiety. For instance, it is known that certain shampoo brands use rabbits to test their products to see if any kind of skin reaction appears. Needless to say, this must be quite a painful procedure for the animals that get skin rashes as a result of the experiment.

However, it cannot be denied that great discoveries have been made through animal testing. Diseases that used to be lethal have now been nearly eradicated thanks to medical research, which has made it possible for us to have medicine that can prevent the spread of such illnesses. A good illustration of this is immunizations, which are now available to most people, in most countries, to be used from the birth, preventing a considerable number of deaths by contracting ailments such tuberculosis or the whooping cough. Unfortunately, none of these advancements would be possible without testing on animals.

To conclude, animal testing is a controversial issue simply because it is a practice that is not completely moral. But I have to advocate for the benefits that this practice has brought to the health and safety of humankind.

(338 Words)

Sample Two-part Question Type

Case 1 - Sample A

Write about the following topic:

The use of recreational drugs is on the increase, especially among young people. Describe the reasons for this worrying issue and provide suggestions to minimize it.

Give reasons for your answer and include any relevant examples from your own knowledge or experience.

Write at least 250 words.

Suggested Plan:

Topic: Use of recreational drugs among young people
Thesis Statement: causes and solutions

Topic sentence: Access of drugs
- **Cause:** Drugs dealers make it easy to get
- **Suggestion:** Check people more thoroughly

Topic sentence: unhappiness
- **Cause:** emotional pain
- **Suggestion:** Provide more support

Recreational drugs are an ever increasing habit for many young people across the world. Not only is this very concerning for society in general, but the effects this has on young people can be debilitating for their future lives. There are two key reasons for this worrying issue, but some measures can help mitigate the problem.

Firstly, a major reason for this increase is how disturbingly easy it is to either buy or get access to drugs these days. Not only are there dealers constantly making themselves available to young people, but the ever growing supply makes drugs cheap as well. For instance, it is known that in most popular parties or night clubs, people can buy practically any drug they wish even when these places are controlled by security. An effective solution for these common situations would be to improve the level of security in such events by increasing the number of guards, thoroughly checking attendees' belongings and denying access to any suspicious people. This measure would considerably decrease the availability, and thus, consumption of illegal substances.

In addition, the current volumes of drug consumption can be attributed to the high levels of dissatisfaction many people experience these days. The dissolution of the family unit, constant and imminent wars, heart break and death are many triggers that make some people want to escape their pain and use substances that will allow them to evade these feelings, even if just for a while. In order to rectify this predicament, families should be more observant of their loved ones and be wary of any changes in behaviour and offer their unconditional support. Likewise, authorities should put more systems in place, which can aid vulnerable people to access help in situations when they may be isolated from their families, such as homeless youngsters, ex-soldiers and unemployed people.

In summary, recreational drugs are certainly having an immense impact on young people because of the increase in use. However, there are several measures that can be taken to minimize and limit the use. Implementing stricter security where drugs are easily available and providing more support will go a long way to helping this issue.

(360 Words, chain structure used)

Case 1 - Sample B

Write about the following topic:

An increasing number of couples have adopted a 'childless' lifestyle over the last decades. What do you think is causing this? What effects will this trend have on society?

Give reasons for your answer and include any relevant examples from your own knowledge or experience.

Write at least 250 words.

Suggested Plan:

Topic: Couples with no children
Thesis Statement: Causes and effects on society

Topic sentence: Causes
- **Reason 1:** busy lifestyle
- **Example:** career focus
- **Reason 2:** no responsibility
- **Example:** more free time

Topic sentence: Positive and negative Effects
- **Reason 1:** Positive, more tax for gov
- **Example:** Australia
- **Reason 2:** Negative, older population

New ways of having a family have come to be more accepted and the old roles of men and women seem to be part of the past. Together with these changes, a new movement of couples who decide not to have children has become more common, introducing a child-free lifestyle. Some of the causes and effects of this trend will be analysed as follows.

Firstly, different reasons can be found when it comes to this trend. To start with, a major cause would be the modern and busy way of living. Life has become much more demanding than 20 years ago. These days, people need to not only have one degree, but ideally pursue a post-degree in order to compete in today's market. For this reason, some couples are too occupied building their careers to consider having progeny. Additionally, many couples prefer to have a more flexible way of life that allows them to travel or partake in activities which children may difficult. I personally have several friends and even family members who have chosen not to have children because they say they are too busy enjoying life without the responsibility it involves to be a parent.

Consequently, this life choice may bring positive and negative effects to society. Governments that provide free welfare with tax-payers' money would benefit from this drift. This is because there would be fewer people in need of social aid, such as childcare allowances. An illustration of this is Australia, where people who have children receive a series of social help such as a baby bonus and all kinds of rebates. However, an inevitable negative impact would be a rising aging population, which would affect the economy of the country in several ways. More stress would be placed on age-care and there would be a higher demand for skilled professionals in any new career paths. An example of this is Japan, where population has decreased by the lowering birth rates.

All in all, it is clear to see why so many people are choosing to have a child-free lifestyle and it is expectable that this trend increase over the next few years. But the consequences need to be addressed in order to prevent social problems in the future.

(373 words)

Case 2 - Sample A

Write about the following topic:

Advertising is the most commonly used tool for companies to sell their products. In what aspects of our life is advertising present? What effects can advertising have on people?

Give reasons for your answer and include any relevant examples from your own knowledge or experience.

Write at least 250 words.

Suggested Plan:

Topic: advertising
Thesis Statement: where is it, what effects does it have on people?

Topic sentence: presence of advertisement
- **Reason 1:** everywhere
- **Example:** internet, TV, roads

Topic sentence: effects on people
- **Effect 1:** Positive, inform customers
- **Example:** sales, special features
- **Effect 2:** Negative, misleading
- **Example:** food

Advertising surrounds virtually everybody in the entire world every day. In fact, we get consumed by advertising without us consciously knowing about it. However, there are specific aspects of our lives in which advertising is more present. Furthermore, there are also certain effects that this can have on people.

To begin with, advertising is very present in every aspect of our lives. Wherever we go or look, we are bombarded by propaganda. Whether we like it or not, advertising is not a choice anymore but compulsory viewing. Companies know that the more presence they have, the more people will feel the need to use their products. For this reason, they have taken possession of every media available to publicize their brand. Examples of this can be found in all kinds of activities we do daily, for instance, doing an internet search will prompt all sorts of commercials on both sides of a webpage and even pop-up windows. When driving, it is possible to notice billboards and banners. Finally, television and radio would not be possible without the support of sponsors who pay channels and stations for promotion.

Nonetheless, the effects of this constant propaganda exposure should not be overlooked. Firstly, it can be beneficial to have access to advertisement. People can get informed about special sales or specific features of different products which can help customers take advantage of these opportunities or get better-informed about a good. On the other hand, it is undeniable that advertising can be quite misleading. Sometimes companies use their media exposure to promote certain products which can be said to have qualities when in reality it may be the opposite case. A good example of this is food, where the products that are publicized the most, tend to be the unhealthiest, such as junk food, or sugary drinks.

In conclusion, it can be affirmed that we are surrounded by advertising wherever we go and the impacts of this constant propaganda exposure can be positive or negative for customers.

(333 words)

Case 2 - Sample B

Write about the following topic:

More and more women have joined the work force in recent years. What reasons do women have to be more professionally driven? What effects does this trend have on their families?

Give reasons for your answer and include any relevant examples from your own knowledge or experience.

Write at least 250 words.

Suggested Plan:

Topic: More women participation in workforce
Thesis Statement: reasons and effects

Topic sentence: why women work more
- **Reason 1:** women's new role in society
- **Example:** politics and business
- **Reason 2:** family needs
- **Example:** cost of life

Topic sentence: effects on society
- **Effect 1:** Positive, more diversity
- **Example:** men and women complement each other
- **Effect 2:** Negative, less quality time with children

All around the world, we have seen a shift in the participation of women in society. What used to be unthinkable has now become the norm, for instance, the US is about to have the first female president. These days women are more career focused than their counterparts 20 years ago. I believe there are various reasons for these changes and inevitably, there will be consequences for society as well.

First of all, it is important to analyse what has caused this movement. One reason women have become more professionally active is the role of women, which has radically changed. Women used to be the carers of the family, responsible for the nourishment and education of children and house chores. Nowadays, more and more women have access to education, which atomically leads to a desire to develop a professional career. Another aspect, is the fact that most households need a double income to support their families. The cost of life has risen considerably in most countries, which has made it almost compulsory for women to have to become professionally active.

From another angle, the effects of these changes can also vary. On the positive side, it can be said that the participation of women in the workforce makes the working environment much more diverse and integral. Female workers have as much or more expertise and knowledge to share and contribute with, and they are the perfect complement for their male counterpart, which may assure a more equitable dynamic work space. Nevertheless, some might worry that having women work more, may bring adverse effects such as the disintegration of the family in extreme cases, or the negligence of children who may be left alone for long periods of time while both parents work.

To sum up, it is clear to see that the increase of female involvement in the work force has been caused mainly by social changes. These can bring both positive and negative effects to society.

(327 words)

ABOUT THE AUTHOR

Daniella Moyla

Daniella is a highly sought after IELTS consultant due to her ability to make IELTS easy for people to understand.

Daniella is a degree qualified English teacher with expertise in ESL, academic English, TOEFL and IELTS preparation.

Born in Chile, English is not her first language which has allowed her to understand the difficulties faced by anyone taking the IELTS exam.

Daniella has written several IELTS training courses which demonstrates her comprehensive understanding of the IELTS and the requirements for achieving a high score.

Her love of teaching also inspires her to continue following her passion of helping as many people as possible pass the IELTS.

I   – introducere
      – ~~sumar~~ prezentare pe scurt.

      – descriere

      – concluzie

                           4 poragrafe

II   plan

     Temo

     Thesis statement

Topic sentence	Topic sentence
Example	Example ~~reason~~
Reason	Reason
	example
	reason

     summary . 250–300 cuv

                4 paragrafe

Printed in Poland
by Amazon Fulfillment
Poland Sp. z o.o., Wrocław